POETRY ESCAPE

Break the silence,
tell your truth.

LANCASHIRE POETS

Edited By Megan Roberts

First published in Great Britain in 2019 by:

Young Writers
Remus House
Coltsfoot Drive
Peterborough
PE2 9BF
Telephone: 01733 890066
Website: www.youngwriters.co.uk

SB ISBN 978-1-78988-502-6
Printed and bound in the UK by BookPrintingUK
Website: www.bookprintinguk.com
YB0404IZ

FOREWORD

Since 1991 our aim here at Young Writers has been to encourage creativity in children and young adults and to inspire a love of the written word. Each competition is tailored to the relevant age group, hopefully giving each student the inspiration and incentive to create their own piece of creative writing, whether it's a poem or a short story. We truly believe that seeing their work in print gives students a sense of achievement and pride.

For our latest competition *Poetry Escape*, we challenged secondary school students to free their creativity and break through the barriers to express their true thoughts, using poetic techniques as their tools of escape. They had several options to choose from offering either a specific theme or a writing constraint. Alternatively they could forge their own path, because there's no such thing as a dead end where imagination is concerned.

The result is an inspiring anthology full of ideas, hopes, fears and imagination, proving that creativity really does offer escape, in whatever form you need it.

We encourage young writers to express themselves and address topics that matter to them, which sometimes means exploring sensitive or difficult topics. If you have been affected by any issues raised in this book, details on where to find help can be found at: **www.youngwriters.co.uk/support**.

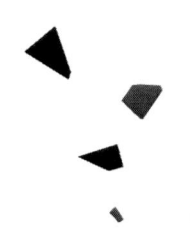

CONTENTS

Jessica Jayne Short (12) — 82
Claudia Barrett (12) — 83
Lizzie McCabe (13) — 84
Ruby Morris (12) — 86
Violet Dunne (11) — 88
Cian Robinson (13) — 89
Emily Grace Scrutton (12) — 90
Lily Mae Rutherford (11) — 92
Joshua Houghton (13) — 93
Jacob Louis Kearsley (12) — 94
Dylan Stephens (12) — 95
Emma Rachel Hoctor (13) — 96
Ben Blackley (12) — 97
Evie Minion-Newby (12) — 98
Ellie Mai McKellen (12) — 100
Brendan Lee Fitzsimmons (12) — 102
Christopher Owen (12) — 103
Findlay Horner (14) — 104
Jasmyn Morris-Holden (11) — 106
Amy Halliwell (12) — 107
Molly Scot-Walker (12) — 108
Ben Shone (12) — 109
Aaron Storey (12) — 110
Toby Runciman (13) — 111
Amelka Zambrzycka (12) — 112
Libby Houghton (11) — 113
Joshua McMahon (13) — 114
Ayeza Athar (12) — 115
Millie Jean Howarth (11) — 116
Josh Papp (12) — 117
Lujain Al Moukayed (12) — 118
Lucy Sherratt (12) — 119
Olivia Rose Killeen (13) — 120
Callum O'Hanlon (12) — 121
Amalia Vogt (11) — 122
Leo Brannan (11) — 123
Alex Lloyd (12) — 124
Edward Whittingham (13) — 125
Jessica Hazel Stocks (12) — 126
Luke Leadbeater (12) — 127
Sophie Patricia Stocks (12) — 128
Alisha McChrystal (13) — 129
Benedict Kayonda (11) — 130

Chloe Jones (12) — 131
Michael Anderton (11) — 132
Layton Openshaw (13) — 133
Azuolas Sinusas (12) — 134
Molly Hacking (12) — 135
Greg Kay (13) — 136

Tarleton Academy, Tarleton

Max Stuart Graham Gilmore (13) — 137

Thomas Whitham Sixth Form, Burnley

Nikola Zygo (16) — 139

Turton High School, Bolton

Beatrix Neary-Taggart (13) — 140
Ava Longworth (12) — 142
Charlie Holt (11) — 143
Tara Jessica Cummings (13) — 144

Unity Academy, Blackpool

Kayleigh Robinson (13) — 146
Leah Carradice (13) — 147

First Day Of High School

I am nice and clean for my first day of school
I have even cut my hair!
Though I'm going to be nervous on my first high school day
It's something I can't bear!

I am wandering the corridors and no one is walking with me
I want to sit in the corner and just weep
I wish I could jump out the window and leap

Lessons are hard, it's not what I'm used to
I don't even know my way around the school
Where is the loo?

I saw a kid sitting on the bench at break
Hey! I know that guy!
So, I plucked up the courage and went to say hi

High school is now fun, now that I'm used to it
Nowadays, when I leave school, I don't want to say goodbye
But, when I do, I want to cry and cry!

Aayan Ali (11)

Eden Boys' School, Preston

Remembrance Day

I see rivers of mud-red blood too
I see nurses helping me and you
I see trenches of blood and fields of mud
The huge bombs dropping to the floor with a thud.

I see wounded bodies crying for help underneath the smoke
They're really saying this war is no joke
I smell smoke, watch dead bodies rot
They will never know if they won the war or not.

I see men fighting and dying
I see people on their knees, crying
I see guns blasting
No, they are not acting.

No, this is definitely not a nightmare
No, it is not a scare
Why could you not spare
All those people who care
Why was it so unfair?

I saw death and destruction
All the blood I could see on the ground
Wear a poppy to remember
All those soldiers who died
In the months between June and November.

You sent young boys out of their homes
Then they died and were treated like gnomes
Some people did really bad things
But they weren't punished for them.

Innocent people who died for no reason
All those people who died in that season
Why did they have to go through pain?
Why couldn't they just gain?

Many things happened in war
Peace was gone
Humility was gone
Relationships broken
All these things happened in war and they were all done.

People ask why we wear a poppy
So we don't copy
Those people who killed normal people.

Families heartbroken
Why couldn't they have spoken
About people's rights
To live life normally?

That is why we have Remembrance Day
So we can say thank you in a special way.

Zayd Badat (12)
Eden Boys' School, Preston

Human Nature

When a person witnesses injustice,
They tend to remain silent,
Yet when they experience it
They are likely to become violent,
As if they are a dog,
That barks non-stop,
Or as if they are a child,
That's been living in the wild

Jealousy
Selfishness
Greediness
Passiveness
All of these creatures have destroyed world happiness

Let us not continue on this disgrace of a path
As it'll lead to Satan's sadistic laugh

We are indeed the best of creation
And we shall unite all strayed nations

Whether we believe in God or not
We shall feed the poor,
Clothe the poor,
And love the poor -
You may ask, "What is 'poor'?"
Well that is up to you to define,
I am greatly sorry but I have forgotten the next line

However it doesn't matter,
As long as we do not allow ourselves to shatter

Human nature shall be restored
And now it is *your* turn to play the next *chord*.

Haadi Ali (12)
Eden Boys' School, Preston

Game Time

In the crowds we go
The population grows
The big game of ball
This cannot be low
Of course, it is high
Oh, it is really a fight
Where two teams come together
And perform on a big night.

This atmosphere is great
This is not a lie
I cannot be late
Or your stomach will be fried
In they come
Out the hole
They stand in a line
In their positions
Off we go, it is a big game of football!

The stadium is sublime
Like you can imagine
The ball will fly
As we will ponder
The sky will flourish
It is bright
With big groups of light
There is no fright.

The grass is green
The centre spot is white
Everybody is keen
Our team will fly like a kite
The whistle is blown!
Thweep! Thweep! Thweep!
It is game time!

Muhammad Patel (11)
Eden Boys' School, Preston

Bloodshed

No head
Bloodshed
Rats fed
57,000 dead
Bayonets red
The soldiers said:

Broken ones and dreadful yawns
Souls had holes and hearts were splintered
Dismembered soldiers buried in sorrow
Opposite blood captures the enemy's joy
While the graves remain in the ash of conflict and still
remain in ruins.

Widowed wives cry
In a second, they all die
Even though they try
They can't relive their sigh.

Machine guns killing warriors as the cowards stay back
No Man's Land causes death in bunches
But still, the trench foot possesses the most horror

Fields were red
Then, someone stays dead

Rest in peace beloved warriors
This is what the soldiers said!

Naail Mirza (13)
Eden Boys' School, Preston

The Suffering

We hear today's news
About countries like Palestine
People who whine
Bombs are falling from the sky.

I said, "Why?"
But I watched a video of mothers cries
And brothers dying
And their bodies frying.

Learn from the Holocaust
Look what humans caused.

This is the suffering
This is bad
Please stop the bickering
We all are sad.

Why are you culprits so thirsty for blood?
Oh people, please end the nonsense for good.

Please think so hard
I hear kindness in your heart
These days will soon be gone
But the worst might come
I'm afraid the message will be too late
It'll all be done
This is the suffering.

Muzamil Shah (12)
Eden Boys' School, Preston

I And Dem

When I look in di mirror:
I call maself de next Einstein - but dem just call me a tramp,
I call ma hair an Afro (like Salah's) - but dem just call it dishevelled,
I call ma colour bronze - but dem just call it burnt,
I call ma beard trendy (like Beckham's) - but dem just call me Fader Christmas
I call ma attire unique - but dem just call it out of place,
I call ma culture vibrant - but dem just call it wild,
I call me house a home - but dem just call it a hut,
I call maself hands-on - but dem just call me a slave.

I call all dis discrimination - but dem just call it: *freedom of speech*.

Zayd Saeed (16)
Eden Boys' School, Preston

To Brexit Or Not To Brexit?

Empty promises from those with power
Yet nearly three years on, still unresolved
Remoaners remain
Brexiteers subsist
Exasperated, we appear to exist

Some say leaving the EU will leave Britain a vassal state
Others say we will be better to separate

What if 'No Deal' means no meal?
How will it affect us? What does it all mean?
Blood boiling, milk curdling, emotions aflare,
What the future holds remains to be seen.

Let bygones be bygones
Is something often said.
Yet, had it not been for Cameron,
We would not be in this mess.

Uthman Shaikh (13)
Eden Boys' School, Preston

Trapped!

I wander through each secluded street,
The towering trees glare over me,
The smell of the plants ripple across the air,
Laughter of the children fills the air.

The repeated noise of each blare creates despair,
The people shouting echoes all around,
As each leaf sways from one side to the other,
A storm blows one after the other.

The bold brick buildings surround me on every corner I turn,
Each bench planted and scattered is filled like a barrier,
There is nowhere to turn,
Nowhere to escape, trapped!

Aadil Dalal (13)
Eden Boys' School, Preston

Remembrance Day

Bombs falling like heavy rain,
Soldiers feeling all the pain,
Running, crawling, jumping high,
Remember the ones who died.

They lie on the ground, dying,
Birds in the sky, flying,
Bullets flying everywhere,
Remember the ones who died.

They squealed when they were dying,
Children and wives crying,
They stood up for our country,
Remember the ones who died.

On that day, when they won,
Three cheers for everyone,
They risked their lives just for us,
Remember the ones who died.

Ahmad Patel (12)
Eden Boys' School, Preston

My Clever Thoughts!

A strange question was posed to me
Can a man create a route in the sea?

My answer was, "It is impossible, never
Can be achieved by a man who is clever."

But, I'm young and it is not my destination
My whole focus is only on my education.

My two friends, who are a pen and a book
These have given me the greatest achievements, have a look.

Great respects to my teachers and my parents
Nice phrases from them coming through my larynx.

Kashif Jamil (11)
Eden Boys' School, Preston

My Luxury Vehicles

In my Lambo, I was driving slow,
In my Merc, I was driving low,
I got a fine for driving quick
And you all know me, I'm just slick.

On Monday, I got a Kawasaki Ninja,
My brother had intentions to injure,
He went to take a nap,
I just bought a chicken wrap.

I let the Ferrari roll,
Just then, I saw Aubameyang score his 90th goal,
After that, I pulled a wheelie
And my mate said, "Really?"

Umar Nadeem (12)
Eden Boys' School, Preston

Arctic

A s the days go by, I get hungrier and hungrier
R eceiving letters which are making me angrier
C annot take the pain anymore
T ake note, you fishermen leave our fish by the shore
I ncreasing global warming is already decreasing our breeding
C autiously, I waddle around the Arctic surviving on those remaining.

Yahya Mahmood (11)
Eden Boys' School, Preston

Faith Is In Your Heart

Faith is in your heart
For you to make the right choice
So you can get that perfect start
It is all because of hope
To reach your dreams
It will never go wrong
It will never go apart
So you can get your answers to why
Keep your hope high
Faith in your heart
Keep the meaning of your life.

Zaki Shah (11)
Eden Boys' School, Preston

Love Your Parents

I love you so deeply Mum and Dad
I love you so much
I love the sound of your voices
I love your smiles
And your thoughtful minds
The joy that you bring to my life every day
I love you today as I have from the start
And I'll love you forever
With all of my heart.

Yacoob Mulla (11)
Eden Boys' School, Preston

October...

October's the month with the smallest breeze
Cyclone winds zooming through the leaves
Trick or treating
On the darkest streets
Boys and girls with raising heartbeats
Everyone dressed up for horror and delight
Remember to be careful on Halloween night...

Ismaeel Mulla (12)

Eden Boys' School, Preston

Brothers In Arms

Brothers in arms
To the songs of war they came
For their mother's arms they cried
For their kings they fought
For they are the forgotten
Soldiers of a war gone by
The toys of an oppressor
But that's the nature of war.

Mohammed Haashir Shafiq (11)
Eden Boys' School, Preston

Football

He kicks the ball really high
It goes high into the sky
Goal! He dribbles for the whole play
Soon, he meets a stranger
He is in some danger
It's a penalty, he shoots with some power
The ball goes up and hits the Big Ben Tower!

Zaid Shaikh (11)
Eden Boys' School, Preston

Football

Whenever I kick a ball on the wall
All I hear are cheers
Some people think I'm crazy
I call myself an enthusiast
Liverpool is my favourite team
The best I have ever seen
Whenever Mo Salah scores
The crowd just roars.

Mohammad Hashim Siddique (11)

Eden Boys' School, Preston

The Statue And The Soldier

Atop a hill, overlooking a lake
There stands a statue in all its glory
Standing proud and tall
The patriotic look on his face
Still as fresh as the day it was made.

A soldier laughing with all his friends
Shows the unwavering confidence
Of a fresh platoon
Making their way to the battlefield
Its patriotic glare not so confident.

Around the soldier, gunfire starts
His stance for glory starting to crumble
The great war around him has now begun.

The statue smashes, falling to the ground
Not the man he was or will ever be again
His stone body ended, only the sediment left.

The soldier is shot, his friends all gone
He loses all hope, his mind is shattered
He hopes they remember him
For who he once was.

Joe Goodstadt (14)
St Bede's RC High School, Lytham

Lamb

Through the fresh, frosty gaze of a crisp spring morning,
I see newborn lambs in the field as I'm yawning.
My heart sinks with the innocent sound of their bleat,
Have these poor animals been bred just to eat?

As soon as these lambs have been brought to the planet,
They have one purpose: to be slaughtered by giants.
An animal's life is as precious as ours is,
No childhood, no future, yes, that they'll sadly miss.

The life that we live is good and full of bliss,
Something the animals will all be forced to miss.
They say think of your body and all that you know,
Does that stop animal agriculture to grow?

The lamb has no voice, it just does as it's told,
Unbeknownst to it, the butcher it will behold.
They go to the field, get ripped away from their mum,
Sit patiently waiting for the spring morning sun.

I prefer seeing animals living and free,
Fulfilled as nature intended them to be.
Not to be manufactured for profit or greed
Or to satisfy man's bloodthirsty and greedy needs.

A mother denied to bring up her little child,
Breeding to slaughter, stolen his right to be wild.

A date with the butcher is this lonely child's face,
A life created and lost to fill up a plate.

Only one special spring will this sweet baby know,
One special spring to play before his life will go.
As he's killed by the stroke of the cruel butcher's knife,
What a senseless, greedy waste of this poor lamb's life.

His ears are ringing with the sound of the loud gun,
He's trying to be calm, thinking of all the fun.
His turn is here as he thinks of his lone mother,
His dying thoughts, they were his sister and brother.

Flinty Haiva Richardson (14)
St Bede's RC High School, Lytham

Our Sixth Sense

I close my eyes when there's too much to handle
Too much to think
Too much to say

I tidy my room as if I'm clearing my mind
I throw things away
Leave old memories behind
Books I never read
Toys torn at the edge
Clothes that do not fit with what society has said

You see there are invisible rules
It's humans' sixth sense
We abide with the rules
We do not cross the fence

Fake messages are spread to embrace ourselves
Our natural skin
Our body shape
But, when we step outside
It turns to hate
Tell us to cover up and conceal our mistakes
We cannot be categorised
We cannot be labelled
But we do it anyway
So why aren't we shameful?

It is very clear to me
From a young point of view
That perfect isn't possible
But the message hasn't gone through
The media is corrupt in so many ways
Immoral writers creating these immoral days

Some say we're all different
Unique with odd gifts
Others say we're the same
Just born adrift
But which one is true?
Who do we believe?
Which religion is right?
What sexuality is wrong?
The questions are endless
And the answers are long

Why don't we feel safe
Being our true selves?
Can't we break the rules for once
And not do what society tells?

Liv Louise Hothersall (14)

St Bede's RC High School, Lytham

Am I Good Enough?

The dangers of a single story
Can ruin one's life
Judging and categorising people
On the way they look
Where they were born
And what they believe

Even in sport, there is anger and pain
Fear and anxiety, something proven to release joy
Leaves people questioning their authority
And asking 'am I good enough?'
They have been categorised, a sign around their neck
Even before the whistle is blown

In work
Where a quarter of our limited time is spent
Discrimination hides and waits to pounce on its prey

He was a young male, fighting for his place
With the added challenge of his beliefs
He said, "I am not Superman." Correct he was
However, the fact that what he had achieved seemed so
drastic
Showed the corruption behind the mask.

She was an elderly woman, categorised as controversial
All she did was sit down
But, because of her skin colour

She was called names that cannot be repeated
All because of the way she looked.

Stereotypes were not there at the start of time
And they will not be there at the end
We created stereotypes and categories together
Yet, they are what tore us apart.

Is it because of the way I look?
Is it because of where I was born?
Is it because of what I believe?

Am I good enough?

Christopher Kelly (14)
St Bede's RC High School, Lytham

The Fourth Of July

Inspired by Riverdale

The fateful day came and went
The one she'd have done anything to prevent
There was a wooden boat
That failed to float.

The girl managed to make it to shore
The boy faced a fate with a lot more gore
And that was the story told
But the real one was about to unfold.

The boy did make it back to the riverbank
And, to be frank
He was looking for a girl
The one with blonde curls.

He was unaware that what he was searching for
Was not waiting for him on the shore
She was taken away by her parents
As she was being aberrant.

The boy didn't die that day
In fact, it was a while until he faced that fate
He set off to the getaway car
But he didn't get that far.

The boy was jumped by a man his dad had hired
But the gun still hadn't been fired

The dad wanted to do it himself
He must have been ever so stealth.

The boy was tied up to a chair
Knowing he didn't have much time to breathe air
Then, there he was, gun in hand
But, as usual, he looked grand.

He held up the gun to the boy's head
The dad watched as the young boy bled
That was the aftermath of July fourth
But I'm the only one who knows about the corpse...

Cara Restrick (12)
St Bede's RC High School, Lytham

The Quiet One

Without malice, they depict me
A girl with no mouth
Too shy, too consumed by quietness
Large eyes in a pale, strained face
Fingers crossed, legs crossed
Avoiding the gauntlet of the toilet block
But then you appear, you smile, you care
Life that day is better than before.

We discuss, we plan, we share
Time flies, we laugh in collaboration
Eyes bright, alive together
Arms linked, legs sauntering.
A girl with a saddened smile, alone in a queue
But then we appear, we smile, we care
Life that day is better than before.

Without thought, they depict us
The group with no 'cred'
Too kind, too steeped in self-awareness
Lacking in the labels' department
Fonder of actual chat than cyber chat
But then we are actually there
We smile, we care
Life each day is better than before.

The quiet one, a grown-up now, Mum
Her daughter, alone, always
Tear-stained, isolated, waiting for a friend
A mother's empathy from one who knows
They will appear, they will smile, they will care
Life from that day will be better than before.

Amelie Morris (14)
St Bede's RC High School, Lytham

It's Not Right

It's not right,
Injustice,
War, bullying,
Racism.

Why can't we learn to love?
Does it matter that people are different from each other?
Can't we stop to think about why we are pursued by hate
and discrimination?
Does it really matter that people are from another nation?

It's not right,
War,
Will it really solve our problems?
Or create new ones?

Racism,
Is it because people are afraid of what they don't
understand or don't know?
Or because we have the need to feel superior and segregate
others?

Bullying,
Is it because we are pressured by our daily obstacles?
Or are we feeling anger, hatred and sadness by an
argument between our closest which gives us the need to
take it out on someone?

Injustice,
Is it because we are unequal to others?
Or because we are older than others and feel we can treat
them differently?

It's not right.

Piotr Kozomaricz (13)
St Bede's RC High School, Lytham

Ice

Ice, thin ice
So slim that we cannot see
How close we are to falling
Through to the Earth's core
Where our hearts will be warmed
And the frost dies
Because there is an existing cure.

However, the cure was not always so clear
Sometimes, it serene to evoke elements of fear
For, next time there is a sea of unknown faces
I'll ignore the silent rupture and hiss inside
As well as imaginary whispers about now
Haven't cleared my morning voice
And show an expression of being falsely satisfied.

Ice, thick ice
So thick that I cannot see the glow of the moon
As I am trapped at the Earth's core
Where my heart is forced to be warmed
Just because there is an existing cure.

Letty Ormerod (14)
St Bede's RC High School, Lytham

Did I Do Enough?

Every day of every week
I come home thinking
What do I have to do now?
Sometimes, it's homework
Sometimes, it's revision
Or sometimes, it's reflecting
On what happened that day.

That girl got bullied by a group of boys
Did I do enough to help?
That teacher shouted at an innocent boy
Did I see if he was okay?
I did a science test today
Did I put enough effort in to do my best?
Some people in this world are less fortunate than us
Can I do enough?

For many days, months and years to come
I will think each and every evening
Did I do enough?
The answer is yes
Whatever happens that day
Remember, you are enough.

Caitlin Murphy (13)
St Bede's RC High School, Lytham

If Only You Had Cared

She grips her chest, struggles to keep the noise in,
Time has passed midnight as teardrops pour down.
Her brain is a drug filled with poison,
Who knows how long 'til she really shuts down?

Voices in her head are uninviting,
Yet she listens and believes every word.
Trying to stay sane is hugely frightening,
You do listen, but she never gets heard.

She says she's an artist, not how you'd think,
For her pens are blades and her paper, skin.
Demons drag her under, she starts to sink,
But what will happen when those demons win?

All you say is 'don't worry', 'don't be scared',
Now she has gone. If only you had cared.

Bismah Ballout (13)
St Bede's RC High School, Lytham

A Football Is Black And White

Football is a sport for all nations and races
But a bitter rival tears teams apart
Games get abandoned and tears run down faces
A sinful beast lies at the heart.

Torched tongues of hooligans hunting the hate
At talent longing for support
Racism, dictator of a near-battered state
A cruel part of the wonderful sport.

From Milan's Kevin-Prince Boateng to Sterling of City
The victims of the ongoing war
Ignorant fans who do not take pity
It's in our hands to teach them the score.

Discrimination deserves a stern red card
We're all referees of the fight
We need to stand up, this is our yard
A football is black and white.

Ashton Taylor (14)
St Bede's RC High School, Lytham

Global Warming

There's a lot of things going on in the world
Poverty and global warming
People say it's just the weather
But it's not.

Evil weather can affect lives
And ecosystems are getting destroyed
The ice caps all because of 'just weather'.

Farmers cannot grow crops
Because of 'just weather'
Animals are losing their habitats
Because of 'just weather'
There must be some change.

Start with the little things
And work up
Try to use little plastic
Don't send waste to landfill
If you can help it
Because 'just weather'
Is changing lives
And not for the better.

Bradley Rhys Clarke (12)
St Bede's RC High School, Lytham

My Life Of Isolation

I'm not the only kid who has dealt with this
I'm not the only kid who will forget what happened
But I am the only kid who knows how I feel
Most days, I walked in thinking, *I've got to hide*
I walked in thinking, *what are they going to do?*
I walked in knowing I would go out alone
I was isolated and distressed
They were rude and cold-hearted
I got hurt most days
Inside and outside
My heart scrunched up under the pressure
I became lifeless and non-communicative
I wanted to die
It's all behind me
But I'll never forget
What they did to me
And my life
It's changed me forever

Jake Moore (12)
St Bede's RC High School, Lytham

Carrot On A Stick

Run before you can walk
Sing before you can talk
Walking along the thin ice of life
In hope not to collapse on the lethal knife,
Wary of our destiny
Becoming our reality
Manipulation causes precipitation
Turning it to a rainy day.

Controlling me until I erupt
Power and authority is now corrupt
Pigs leapt, but the carrot still dangled in his face
Toxic fumes burned within that airspace
All his labours had been returned to dust
But, in his head, this hierarchy needed to adjust
So the farmers were his puppet
And he was their master.

Lynsey Grogan (14)
St Bede's RC High School, Lytham

School Week Poem

Monday, Tuesday
Always stressed and nervous
Watching the clock every second until 3:15

Wednesday, Thursday
Worn out and tired, anxious for the day ahead
Feel like I'm in a dream because I'm so tired
Everything just happens around me

Friday
Relieved and excited
Planning what I'm going to do at the weekend
When I get let out, I feel free

Saturday, Sunday
Goes as fast as the wind
Start to get nervous for the week ahead
Tests, homework, speeches, every week for five years.

We never get a break.

Louise Eddleston (13)
St Bede's RC High School, Lytham

Red

Red, a passionate colour,
Known for its shades:
Lighter or duller.

Red resembles many things:
Fire trucks, cherries, blood,
Lipstick, even a rooster's wings.

Red, even in some flags:
Great Britain, Poland, Portugal,
Germany, Spain and France.

Red, associated with anger,
Watch someone's face steam up,
Frustrated with maths because you don't know the answer.

Red, an all-round colour.

Frazer Harrison (12)
St Bede's RC High School, Lytham

Football Equality

Every weekend, I watch the game
All the players just playing for fame
Nobody cares about their outside life
Or if they need a week off because of their ill wife.

If they do have a day off, what is their pay?
It's all the fans blaming them for the delay
As well, if you ever go to a game
You will see discrimination
By people throwing inflatable bananas at players
Who they don't like
Do you think that's right?

Charlie Ogden (12)
St Bede's RC High School, Lytham

No Strings Attached

A puppet on a string follows every command
From the puppet master above
With all the power in his hands.

Performing is the only thing they are able to do
Whilst the strings are attached
No one sees the suffering they all have to go through.

Ordinary people just see a puppet on a string
But small voices like his, hear
"Break the chains, I'll do anything!"

Esther Dickason (13)
St Bede's RC High School, Lytham

Bullying

Bullying is not okay
Bullying is not fine
Bullying is not a joke
Bullying is serious

Bullying is a problem
A problem we can fix
Bullying makes people depressed
Bullying makes people hurt

Bullying is not funny
Bullying is not a laugh
Bullying makes people's lives miserable
Bullying, change it now!

Bella Dixon (12)
St Bede's RC High School, Lytham

Monday

M aybe this day isn't
O ur favourite, but
N ever forget that every
D ay is a new opportunity
A nd only
Y ou can make it count.

Abby Malone (12)
St Bede's RC High School, Lytham

Consumed

When they ask what I'm afraid of, I lie.
I can't expose you, you're mine.
I climb the barrier of insanity,
Ride the waves of despair each day.
I don't know how to live with you,
Yet I don't know how to live without.
My capturer, my torturer, my lover, my friend,
Your noose tightens around my neck,
Yet you never seem to let me go.
Free me, I plead. You punish me, I bleed.
You chew me up and spit me out,
I'm no use to you, just let me out.
Trapped in the walls that I built on my own,
I've nowhere to escape, no place to call home.
I'm my own perpetrator, you are my saviour.
Allowing me to let out the voices, the screams, the pain
In the form of a red stream that echoes
The voices, the screams, the pain
As the crimson paints the clean floor.
The whole world is silent, yet the sounds are unbearable.
The sights are overwhelming, but not worth seeing.
You've finally let me go, this is it, farewell,
For I'll be better off dead,
Than living in this hell.

Kimberley Entwistle (17)
St John Rigby College, Orrell

Time Can Only Watch

Upon the planes of existence, the gods were gathered
together, impatient in their divinity.
I watched these tall pillars quarrel, Mother Nature cried,
"This must stop!" Her voice,
Oh, her voice, a euphony of squawks and screeches. From
her crown flowed rivers,
From her arms clung lush forests, alive with creatures from
far and from wide.
"All will be well sister." Turning, I saw a human man gesture
to his earth.
A clap of thunderous laughter, "For this is progression and it
is good"

I sighed deeply. A millennium passed.

Clangs of metal and thick plumes of smoke brought me
back to reality again.
The world was much changed, dark towers rose up to choke
the green
And I watched as the god of ice wrung water from his
mighty form.
His features slipped into rivers which gathered in the skirts
of
The goddess of the sea. They begged me to stop this but
The human smiled, "This is progression and it is good."

I bowed my head. A century passed.

The humans, now mad from their power, turned to guns, to violence,
Picking off Mother Nature's wailing children; one by one, they fell.
The humans were merciless, tearing away at Mother Nature
Until she was all but dust and ash, barren and fruitless.
The gods of sea and ice at last collided into one.
"This is progression and it is good."

I wiped away a tear. A decade fell away.

The sun god, now scorched the earth below, and all dams broke
as the sea goddess surged upwards, drowning the poisonous dystopia.
From every direction, children ran.
The human faltered as his own child ran to him.
He begged me for another chance. But I simply laughed
"But this is progression and it is good."

Minutes and seconds slipped through my fingers.

The Earth below was a wasteland and my ancient hands began to
Fade; the clockwork within me clanging to a definite stop.
The fearful human whimpered regretfully; petrified.
"What will you say, when your children ask why?"

The decimated world slipped under the waves.
"Why you didn't act while you still had me?"

"While you still had time?"

Orla O'Donnell (17)
St John Rigby College, Orrell

Solitude's Saviour

And it is through the streets I wander
Like a lonely, helpless child.
As my feet take steps whilst my mind runs behind
With the shouts of the past running wild.

No one can see how lost she is
As they walk past in the streets. Alone.
Blue eyes like a storm, needing its calm
And someone to take her home.

But no one can seem to see the loss
Or how she wishes she could be found
Her blue dress dragging along the floor
Its weight pulling her to the ground.

Will they ever see, she wondered
Just how lost I am?
She grabs the tails of her coats and skirts
"Oh please, can you help me ma'am?"

A hand grabs hers and whispers a chance
She no longer needs to hide
"Lost child, I'm here to take you home."
And begins to look up the mountainside.

Alisha Tait (16)
St John Rigby College, Orrell

This Strange Land

Red, darkening sky lit by dwindling sun
Green no longer, burned beige, water runs
Blue nights, too far from stars or magic
Yellow long gone, not much grows on
This strange land that smells awfully unusual
Empty ground, cracking like a breaking spine
Needles stretch out through colossal mines
Air so thick, it chokes the skies
Night cradles it like desert snakes around
This strange land where fire burns
Ice exists, not even as a forgotten myth
Earth burns brash, bursting into flames
Water trickles, movements scarce and stiff
Deep through dark holes, black like
This strange land scattered with eyes as
Black as vacant seas of dust
Dark and lonely were these creatures' views
Gaping souls stare into the other for hours
Remote and alien, not only to me, but each other in
This strange land, they have
War in their nature, boiling, futile feuds
Blood gushing in and out of their veins
Merciless, spilling anger from hollow orbs
Crazed, animalistic language speaks nonsense despite
This strange land

They play with tongues of orange and red and
Blue, from the dogs of Hell below, not
Born into madness, but creating it
Smile in the face of disaster, for they aren't to live in
This strange land for much longer, but it seems they
Love the fire and the disaster
Blinded by the media
Hypnotised by propaganda
Wild and living in denial, they smile about
This strange land
Do they condone this madness?
Do *we* condone this madness?
Continue to say this isn't real when
We are continuing to live on
This strange land
That we choke and call
Earth.

Tegan Gage (16)
St John Rigby College, Orrell

Anti-Social Media

Social media, who cares anyway?
The answer is you, me, friends and family.
Nobody thinks of the impact every day
Hundreds of innocent lives lost
Because of careless name-calling.

This is for the young souls that are lost
In a bid to impress the audience
Followers that they swear they know.
Everybody can see that they never learned the importance
Of loving yourself before you can love somebody else.

She skips meals to become thin,
The comparisons to other girls clouding her reality.
Smiling, waving, laughing,
Everybody says they love that grin,
Although she's screaming for help,
Unfortunately, ignored again.

He knows that he can't compete; he's weak,
Mentally and physically, he's hurting.
Male suicide rates are increasing,
But they still call him a freak.
He's worried that he'll just become a number
Once he's gone.

You may think this issue is here to stay,
That it can't be helped or managed.

But, maybe, give somebody a compliment today,
Let's fix this problem together as a generation.

Nobody stressed the importance of self-love,
It's the total opposite to self-loathe.
The comments and likes, ignore all of the above,
The only person you should impress is you and only you.

Cara Gaskell (17)
St John Rigby College, Orrell

Tin Man

Sat on a couch, the majority settle,
coffee in hand, food in lap, news blaring.
Disaffected feelings, armour as thick as metal,
staring blank-eyed, pretending to be caring.
They watch, stuffing their mouths, it's not sinking in,
eyes wide, skin untouched with hearts made of tin.

The commute to work is treacherous,
try not to trip on the homeless, drop a penny as you pass.
Spare change? Some food? Don't listen to what they ask,
keep hold of your belongings, there's trouble on the train,
stealing to stay alive doesn't matter
when you're thinking with your brain.

If there's suffering, you shouldn't care unless you see it,
damsel in distress, don't mess, let it sit.
Don't react, think fast and turn your head,
keep away those plaguing thoughts of dread.

Don't think about the girl you saw on her knees,
begging for her chance to be free.
Turn your head from the boy who was wounded,
don't think about how his life concluded.

But, what happens when trouble comes for you?
Will people turn a blind eye too?
Being left alone with your thoughts is mental detonation,
feeding the feelings of self-doubt and devastation.

But, in the end, metal melts, glass breaks;
it is then that your heart will start to ache.

Lizzie Wood (16)
St John Rigby College, Orrell

Coemeterium

Why do we come here
every year, like clockwork?
Is it out of respect?
No, it is because we,
all of us,
refuse to let go.
The time we had exists
only in memory,
the love we had is replaced,
replaced by a slab of marble or stone.
We polish it out of love,
place flowers before it
to represent our love
and carve words into it
to express our love -
to leave something behind.
A name,
a date,
a mark.

Jocelyn Howarth (16)
St John Rigby College, Orrell

Intermission

The sun's warm glow finds its way on my face,
And for a second, sat in my bus seat,
I'm free from worries that are commonplace,
These moments come seldom and are a rare feat,
But grant us time from the tired old briefcase.

Harry James Jones (17)
St John Rigby College, Orrell

Running From Yourself

England was always a bright place for me
A place of joy and hospitality
But with every good package, there is a price
A massive game of chance, rolling the dice
Then you always roll snake eyes
And then there is an evil prize.
Day upon day, minds mentally shatter
Bing, bang, bosh, batter
And it flips the way people live
Such as the boy who went to a school full of judicial villains
Who judged him on his body, his looks, his lifestyle
His anxiety.

Every day the boy would weep and flood his bedroom with tears
Burning his floor with hellish fears
He walked along the mountain path with a grey face
And never paid attention to the Earth laughing at his race
The boy still went to school because his mother wanted him to be a success
But the only success the boy received was the failure of his confidence
He ran and ran from his persona carrying a knife
And sat and listened to Satan insulting him
The deprivation of love was growing too strong
As the boy was beaten by his abusive mum
His only chance was his dad

But he'd left the country with almost everything they had
He ran more and more as the storm brewed
And decided to drop out of school.
The child's mother found out and erased him from the house
But a lick of happiness shone
As the sweetest girl who didn't whine
The happiness conveyed for a while until July
The boy collapsed as he found out the bad news
That his best friend was sent beyond the grave
The boy grew anorexic and lost his thanatophobia
Bang! Running, running from the beast
The roar and scraping of its teeth
As hissing sound rang, his depression throbbed and
aggression thrived
And the curses and spurs of violent verses
Crumbled and tumbled the boy's mumbles
And stabs and jabs from ridiculous mental crabs
The grass caressed his feet
And he stared into the sunset
Feeling good to be free and exclaiming
"I no longer have to run from me!"

Parees Lakhman (13)

St Joseph's RC High School & Sports College, Horwich

Remember Me

"When you are rich and famous,
promise to remember me," he joked.
"I promise," she giggled
and smiled as her uncle spoke.
They exchanged their love yous and goodbyes
and the next week flew by.

The girl was at home, getting ready for school.
That was until a knock at her door
echoed through the room.
Her mother went over to answer the door.
"No!" she cried and fell to the floor.
The girl ran over to see what was wrong,
there stood her aunt and Uncle George.

"Stevie's dead, your uncle..."
The girl's aunt frowned, misery and all.
"No..." the girl's eyes began to water
and she hugged herself,
her father's screams filling the halls.

That day still replays in her head,
every night before she goes to bed.
"Remember me," said he
"When you're rich and famous.
Promise to remember me?"
"I promise, I truly do," said she.

They all wore black and arrived in a black car,
crowds of misery coming from afar.
"Not him, it cannot be him!" a lady cried.
A man came over to keep her calm.
Well, at least he tried.

The family followed behind the coffin,
which the men carried.
His husband scoffed, "No, not him,
the one whom I married..."
The mother stayed quiet, numb inside.
It was like her feelings were stolen by the tide.

The niece of the man in the coffin
clutched onto her father,
the brother of the man.
"It's too soon," muttered the mother.
"Way too soon," cried the brother.

A week had passed since that day
and she still questioned why he left that way
"Oh dear uncle, why didn't you stay?"

Julia Davis (12)
St Joseph's RC High School & Sports College, Horwich

Bullying

Why bully?
Why pick on someone?
Why make them feel small?
Why make them inadequate?

Well, let me tell you more
You wouldn't like it if
They sniggered at you when you walked by
Or passed notes around with tales of you
Or maybe made you feel like you want to cry
Or kicked or punched or pulled your hair

Why bully?
Why make them feel sad?
Why make people feel like
No matter what they do
That it's not good enough?

Let me tell you more
You wouldn't like it if no one was your friend
You wouldn't like it if no one stuck up for you
I bet you wouldn't like it if you went home
To horrible text messages.

I am called Anya
I was bullied five months ago
And this is how it made me feel

Words can hurt
They make me feel emotional
When I haven't done anything bad
But words can hurt the most
It starts as a joke
And ends up as a threat
Why can't you just leave me alone?

It's not my fault that I'm not in your group
It's not my fault that I'm not in your set
It's not my fault that I'm not in your clique
I just want to be left alone
I just want to be me!

Your words are so hurtful
Your words are so painful
I even hear them
As I lie in my bed at night

Why did the horror have to start?
Bullies, everywhere I go
I heard footsteps behind me
I knew they were coming my way
It was all a nightmare for me
But, to them, it was all good fun.

I know I am different from you
And everyone else
But it is not a reason to bully me.

Kiara Chapman (12)
St Joseph's RC High School & Sports College, Horwich

You Are You!

I'm who I want to be
Not the names I get called to my face
Like I'm a big disgrace
When I get called names behind my back
I try to laugh it off
I know who I really am
And I know I don't need someone
To be ruining my day
And I should use it to boost my day
By saying that I'm strong, brave and other things
But it isn't that easy.
I know I do wrong
But if I can stop myself
From saying nasty things to sly people
Then why can't other people?
I know the difference between right and wrong
So why do people think they're different
And that they don't have to be kind?
I'm not the names people put in my pocket on a note
I'm the person my friends and family adore
No one was born to be liked by everyone
But to be nice and loyal to the people who care
When people say 'sticks and stones may break my bones
But words will never hurt me'
But they do hurt and I would rather
Have my bones broken than be called nasty names!

I just think to myself
If they can call me and I don't rise to it
Then I'm the better and bigger person.
I can tell someone to get rid of it and not be scared
And I can help others with the same problem as me.

Phoebe McChrystal (11)
St Joseph's RC High School & Sports College, Horwich

Why Me?

Do you have friends?
Do they trust you?
Do you trust them?
Have they ever upset you?
If they have ever upset you
Then just take a step back and think
Why do I stay with them?

The name they call you
The time they laughed at you
The time they left you alone
The time they ripped your work
And got you in trouble for something they did
But yet, you still call them your best friend!
No one should be treated this way
So, why are you?
That is not a best friend.
You are a kind, caring, inspirational person
And you deserve better.
Bullying is not something you should be experiencing
Just remember one thing
This is not your fault!
You are the bigger and better person
So stop letting them knock you back down
Each time you start to get back up again.
Why are you going through this?

They got hold of your phone number
And started texting you mean and nasty messages
You go home every day, crying with tears
And you spend your time with the names they called you
Running through your head.
You question yourself all the time
You keep it all inside and hide your tears!
Maybe you should question yourself
Why? This is bullying and it needs to stop!

Erin Hughes (12)
St Joseph's RC High School & Sports College, Horwich

You Are Unique And Special

Don't let anyone bring you down.
Even if they want to kick you in the stomach,
You get back up again.
Doesn't matter what your race is, sexuality,
Whether you're fat or skinny,
You are unique!

Stand up to the people who want to inflict hate on you,
They just have problems.
The only way they can solve them is to bully people.
The rhyme 'sticks and stones'.
One line says 'words will never hurt me'
That's wrong because words do hurt.
You are special!

Treat others as you want to be treated.
Some people feel depression and anxiety
Our genes don't determine who we are,
We all look the same inside.
We all have the same organs,
The most important is the heart.
The organ that determines how we feel.
We all have the ability to climb up into the sky
And dream and reach for that star
That we want to achieve.
Our heart and love for people is what matters

Don't sit at the back of the classroom
Scared to ask a question
Because you're afraid of getting it wrong
Don't be scared,
You are unique
And most importantly, special
More special than anyone can be!

Emily Rose Davies (11)
St Joseph's RC High School & Sports College, Horwich

The Journey To Freedom

The journey on the boat tightens the knot
The knot in my stomach from the anxiety in my body
People closing in on me while they pray
For their own lives to be kept instead of thrown away
The boat, the boat decided if I was going to live
The boat, the boat decided to help me flee
This could be the end.

Every breath I take feels like it's worth a million
My mind flashes back to before this all began
To the time when I was happy
When everyone was happy.
The boat, the boat decided if I was going to live
The boat, the boat decided to help me flee
This could be the end.

It feels like I have been here forever
Just waiting for the boat to tip over
And for us all to go down with it
I'm living on borrowed time, I've lost everything
And I won't be able to get it back
It will never be the same, no matter how hard I try.
The boat, the boat decided if I was going to live
The boat, the boat decided to help me flee
This could be the end.
The end of my suffering and pain
The end of my nightmares

The end of trauma
The end of my life...

Ava Prescott (12)
St Joseph's RC High School & Sports College, Horwich

Wrong

The scars on her wrist tell a story
A story of who she was
But not who she is
No one.
She's no one but the freak at the back of the class
Or the shy girl who's last to be picked for football
The girl who sits at the dinner table but never eats
The girl who stares at the ceiling at night
And hopes that tomorrow isn't the same as today...

But it is
The same school, the same people,
The same names shouted across the yard.
Every day, the same as before.
The day before, the same as the next
The monsters that come with the words
Are what scarred her the most.
Depression
Anxiety
Those are the real monsters
Those are what keep you awake at night.

A few years pass
The girl at the back of the class is now a different person
The girl who was last to be picked for football
Now has a husband and kids.

The girl who sat at the dinner table but never ate
Has a good job, a good house and a good life
All she had to do was remember
They were wrong.

Sylvie Angel-Williams (12)

St Joseph's RC High School & Sports College, Horwich

We Are One Together

Do you know?
Know what?
Know about bullying and racism?
No, why?
Let me explain...

Bullying is disgraceful
Same with racism
No one wants it

At school, in public or online
Bullying is an issue, let me explain
Bullying, who wants it? *No one!* Good.
Bullying can cause injuries
Depression and even death
People bully because they think others are weird
Look different, act differently
But actually, we seven billion are one
One in a person
And one with God.

I know that not everyone believes in God
But respect others with the respect you could expect
In a utopia land
No depression, injuries, but no
We get treated the same
No matter what happens.

At school, public or online
Racism is a loud thing
Racism is bad, bad, bad, bad
No one wants it, do you?
We are one
Don't judge people by the colour of their skin
This is wrong, stop it now

Don't forget, we seven billion are one together.

Joshua Lamplugh-Wood (12)
St Joseph's RC High School & Sports College, Horwich

Friends

Friends are special
Friends are the best
Friends are like gold.
Sometimes, they are better than family
Sometimes, they are the ones you need most
Sometimes, they are the ones who stick by you through thick and thin.
But, do you treat them the way they treat you?
Don't push your friends away too soon because, sometimes, you never get them back
How much do your friends really mean to you?

Friends are caring
Friends are loving
Friends are helpful
Sometimes, they can be all you need
Sometimes, they can make everything seem okay
Sometimes, they know just what to do to brighten your day
How much do your friends really mean to you?

Do you treat your friends as special?
Do you care and respect them?
Do you treat them like gold?
My friends are better than family
My friends make everything okay
My friends know just what to do to brighten my day
I know how much my friends really mean to me.

Megan Poole (12)
St Joseph's RC High School & Sports College, Horwich

My First Day Of High School

It was my first day of high school,
Was I nervous or excited?
I wasn't really sure,
but one thing is certain,
Homework would be a lot more.
I had my dark blue blazer, my new black skirt, black shiny
shoes and a new white shirt.
The teachers were welcoming,
The second I walked through the gates,
It was very, very busy but I could still find my mates.
I still had maths, English, science and history too,
But there were still many subjects that I'd yet to do.
At primary school, I started at five to nine,
But now I'm at high school, it's at an earlier time.
After a couple of weeks in, I got used to the school,
I knew what was expected and I knew all the rules.
I have a lot more independence now such as walking home,
But sometimes I stay later, and have netball in the dome.
I left primary school at the top of my game,
But now I've reached high school, I'm starting all over again.

Mia Walters (11)
St Joseph's RC High School & Sports College, Horwich

You Take It All Away

No more!
No more holding back!
You, you take it all away
You, you take all the good things
And replace them with the worst things.
No kid should come out and find out
That one of their family members are gone.
No kid should come home and find out
That their mum has gone to see her best friend's grave.
No kids should wake up in the morning
And find out that their mum has gone to the hospital
And that she might die in the next forty-eight hours.
No kid should have to go and see their mum
And say goodbye, knowing that it might be
The last thing that they might say to her.
Kids should come home and have their mum and dad there
To say, "How was your day?" or that they love you
Or that they made your favourite thing for tea.
Kids should wake up in the morning
And their mum and dad should be there
To see them and say good morning.
That is how it should be.

Jessica Jayne Short (12)
St Joseph's RC High School & Sports College, Horwich

Where Did It All Go Wrong?

Where did it all go wrong?
I used to have a job, a home, a family, a car, a bed
All of that is gone
Every single bit disappeared into thin air
It all started two years ago, when I lost my job
I didn't know what to do when I found out
I froze like a rabbit in headlights.

My job gave me security, colleagues, friends, I was the boss
The car gave me luxury, transport,
Now I walk in tattered clothes
My home gave me shelter from the weather
Now, I sleep on park benches and shop doorways
The money meant eating in fancy restaurants
Now, I scrabble in bins or I beg.

As people walk past, they don't realise
How lonely and unwanted you feel
Cut off and only my memories in my mind
Where did it all go wrong?
I am homeless, no one to call, chat or play
The cold, wet atmosphere freezes my heart
And I shiver in fear
There is no future for me.

Claudia Barrett (12)
St Joseph's RC High School & Sports College, Horwich

Looking Down On Me

It isn't right
Can't deal with what's wrong
The way they look at me
They're not doing anything about it
The teachers
Not taking control
Getting pushed to the back of class
Everywhere I go
People are staring
I feel so shallow, so alone.

When I get home
Straight to my room
The messages coming through
'You're ugly', 'you're fat'
I cry myself to sleep
Can't control how I'm feeling
They just aren't helping
I feel so alone
I'm just a kid
I can't take it on my own.

Waking up so low
Finding a sticky note on my blazer
Do they think I'm too fat?
Too crazy?
I don't know

Help me, please!
The girls at school
They don't get it
I've not said anything
Just one little rumour
And you're treated like dirt
It isn't right.

Lizzie McCabe (13)
St Joseph's RC High School & Sports College, Horwich

Perfect To Me!

Inspired by 'Perfect' by Anne-Marie

You don't need make-up
No need to cover up
Have your own independence
Don't look like a Barbie doll
Everybody wasn't made the same.

Baggy jeans, long T-shirts
Tight jeans, short cropped T-shirts and vests
You don't need to impress
Oversized hoodies, fluffy socks
Cropped hoodie, latest expensive trainers
Comfy, uncomfortable.

Not into fancy cars
I'm rocking baggy jeans
Don't take pictures of everything I do
'Cause that's not being myself
Hair in a messy bun, trackie bottoms
I wish my legs were bigger, bigger than NYC
'Cause you're perfect to me.

You don't need make-up
No need to cover up
Don't hide your beautiful face
Everybody isn't the same

No need to look like a Barbie doll
Long, baggy T-shirts are good enough.

Ruby Morris (12)

St Joseph's RC High School & Sports College, Horwich

Labels Are For Clothes Not People

Person reading this, know that you are strong
Powerful and beautiful in your own special way
And I'm going to prove that to you today
Words hurt, they cause pain and make you feel ashamed
But those words aren't true
This poem tells you many things
Not being the same like twins
We judge a book by its cover
All from one look at each other.

That person's fat, that person's thin
But who really knows the person within?
That person's black, that person's white
We are all fighting the same fight.

She has autism,
He has Down's syndrome
She has dyspraxia,
He has dyslexia
Labels, labels everywhere
I'm not sure anyone cares.

Labels are for clothes
Not made for you and me
We should all try to be one
Stop the labels, everyone.

Violet Dunne (11)

St Joseph's RC High School & Sports College, Horwich

Dear Devil

Do you know what causes war?
No, neither do I, but here are a few examples:
It starts with ageism, racism
These kill hundreds, even thousands
Stop, consider words and actions
Because people take their own lives
Thoughts and feelings take over
And the hellish act comes alive
But the real devil is you, only you control the demon
Don't pull the trigger, don't swipe the knife
Every day, a single person has over 100 thoughts
And over sixty-seven feelings
And 75% of them are horrible things
Suicide is not an option, you tell that devil
"No! I won't let you win!
You aren't going to take another life
This one's mine to live
You took months of my life I'll never get back
But I'm living every last second of my life!"

Cian Robinson (13)
St Joseph's RC High School & Sports College, Horwich

Like A Girl!

"You run like a girl,"
I heard them say.
She started crying
Then ran away.

A teardrop ran down her face,
Don't be ashamed,
No!
'Like a girl' is not a bad thing.
You do run like a girl
You *are* a girl.

Just because you're a girl,
Doesn't mean you mean less than them,
You are still a person,
You have a heart,
You have a soul,
You're worth the same as them
They are just jealous.

People think 'like a girl' is a bad thing,
It sounds like a bad thing,
But you're doing it right,
Keep going!

So the next time someone says,
'Like a girl', say.
"Why is that an insult?

I am a girl,
And I am proud!"

Emily Grace Scrutton (12)
St Joseph's RC High School & Sports College, Horwich

Bullying Hurts!

People are suffering every day
From what other people say
Your actions can cause pain
Amongst others around you.

Crying, hurting every day
All because of you
The things you say, the things you do
Can change someone's life.

If you're a bully, you need to stop
Causing people trouble actually causes tears
It makes people feel unwanted in this world
So think, are you a bully?

You can make people scared for life
All these feelings crammed up inside them
Stop being horrible and disrespectful
In the end, you'll be the one hurting.

If you are a bully, do you feel guilty?
If so, change and say sorry
You may have anger stored inside, but
In the end, only you can change yourself.

Lily Mae Rutherford (11)
St Joseph's RC High School & Sports College, Horwich

Four Years Ago...

It all started four years ago
When all I said to him was no.
Getting punches thrown at me
For just one word.
Bottled it up for all those months...
That's it, enough's enough!
Why do I have to go through
All this pain over just one game?
All these bruises and cuts
But teachers just say, "No ifs or buts."

I don't know what to do with my life anymore
While my whole body is so sore.
Everybody just staring at me
None of the teachers have any hope in me.
All of the other kids with all their fancy shoes
And me, sat here with nothing to lose.

Why do I have to try so hard
To fit in with everyone else?
All I am is a normal kid
With a normal life
And a normal house!

Joshua Houghton (13)
St Joseph's RC High School & Sports College, Horwich

Speak Out

I didn't want to tell anyone
My pain was stabbing me
I can't even describe how it felt
I nearly took my life
They tried to hide me with my fears and my anxiety
I would lie awake at night
That was when it hit me
I would worry about what would come tomorrow
I would wash away the tears from my face
I would come back stronger
I would try to hide the scars
And I would believe
And now I have spoken out
They have been done for it
So I advise you: speak out!

I know how it feels to be lonely
There are many things that can solve it
My scars are still with me
My life leading on
I am who I am and I am proud
I have proved that I can be strong!
We can be strong!

Jacob Louis Kearsley (12)
St Joseph's RC High School & Sports College, Horwich

Stop Bullying

Bullying is bad
It makes you sad
So I talked to my dad
My mum told me to have faith
But I couldn't because I wasn't even safe
Because it was too late.
I was already being treated as bait.
If you think I'm going to the hall of fame
Then I think you're for the blame
I'm not tough
When someone fights me
I feel like I can't get a punch in
And that's why adults give you love
And, when it's over, you feel as light
And as white as a dove
As you feel above the clouds
So, don't be sad
Don't be bad
Be a lad
Don't give in to people calling you
Small like a rat or really fat
Stop bullying
Be a mate before it's too late.

Dylan Stephens (12)
St Joseph's RC High School & Sports College, Horwich

Different World

All we know
left untold
Beaten by a broken dream
Nothing like what it used to be
We've been fighting our demons just to stay afloat
Been building our castle just to watch it fall
Been running forever just to end up here once more
And now we know
This is not the world we had in mind
But we've got time
We are stuck on answers we can't find
But we have time
And, even though we might have lost tonight
The skyline reminds me of a different time
This is not the world we had in mind, but we've got time

Take me back
Back to the mountainside
Under the Northern Lights
Chasing the stars
But we both know that
This is not the world we had in mind.

Emma Rachel Hoctor (13)
St Joseph's RC High School & Sports College, Horwich

My Insecurities

I feel like everyone hates me when I am alone
The voices don't help me either
It's like when you are with your friends
You are in the safe zone
But it gets very melancholic when alone
The voices are like a tumour
And, the more alone you are
It starts to swell and you become insecure
And think that all your friends
Will neglect you the next day.

It feels like you should be ashamed of your body
The way you look and how others see you.
You start to feel like you shouldn't be a part of society
But you have to think about your family and friends
Since you think they are the only people
Who make you, but they just use you.

Ben Blackley (12)
St Joseph's RC High School & Sports College, Horwich

Fox Poaching

We live in fear
We hide underground
We feel scared
We have already lost one
We don't know how long we can last

The cubs cry
The cubs are starving
The cubs dream
The cubs have never been outside
The cubs are scared
The cubs miss their mum.

Humans drive cars
Humans kill us
Humans cut down trees
Humans have no feelings
Humans save other animals, but not us
Humans, why?

Humans say, "What does the fox say?"
But no human says
"How does the fox feel?"

We live in fear
Scared to go out

Most of us went to the city
Most get run over by cars.

Humans don't care about us.

Evie Minion-Newby (12)
St Joseph's RC High School & Sports College, Horwich

Friends

Friends can be good
Friends can be bad
It doesn't matter
What friends you've had.

Friends can be fake
Friends come in time
It doesn't matter
It's up to you!

Friends can be good
Friends can be bad
It doesn't matter
What friends you've had.

Friends, friends
Best friends, enemies
No matter who they are, be nice
Because two wrongs don't make a right!

Friends can be good
Friends can be bad
It doesn't matter
What friends you've had.

Good friends, bad friends
Fake friends, true friends

Always trust your inner self and remember
Choose the right friend!

Ellie Mai McKellen (12)
St Joseph's RC High School & Sports College, Horwich

When Winter Comes Around

It's that time of year when it snows and sleets
The shiny snow sparkles on rooftops
Prancing and dancing down from the sky.

When winter comes around
The snow grows as it cascades down the local mountain
The robins still tweet peacefully like a church choir
As the tranquillity makes you relax.

On the 24th of December, whispering and rustling
Floating down onto your rooftop
With his sack of sparkles and joy.

When winter comes around it is nail-bitingly cold
The people on the local street were witnessing
Incessant, grotesque and horrid weather.

When winter comes around
The magic suddenly begins...

Brendan Lee Fitzsimmons (12)
St Joseph's RC High School & Sports College, Horwich

The Consequences Of War

Poppies are red
Violets are blue
But, in modern warfare
There is only red.

The colour red says a lot
People see it as a colour of love and passion
But there's another side to the devious colour
Red for blood, red for fear, red for death.

That is all that war is
Death for the sake of death
When you think of WW1, WW2,
Iraq, Japan, America,
They all share one thing: death.

My message is, whether it's bullying or fighting
Any type of violence, stop and think
Is this the right thing?
Your words are more powerful than anything else
Speak up against violence, make your voice heard.

Christopher Owen (12)
St Joseph's RC High School & Sports College, Horwich

Why?

Why are they always fighting
Never any talking
Predators are biting
The injured can't be walking
All about politics
All about what they've said
Enemies can be critical
Everyone is dead.

The sound of people crying
Lots of men are dying
All because of what that person said
Dead
Shooting, screaming, shouting
They're all going to die
For their countries, they are fighting
Why?

Bombs go off
Lights go out
No more cries
No more shouting
Everything is calm
The war is over
Families at home
Or staying alone

Their dad's not coming home
Why?

Findlay Horner (14)
St Joseph's RC High School & Sports College, Horwich

The Hunter's Gun!

The animals are scared
From the gunshot they heard
Pow! One's dead while the others fled
Their lives fade away, now each one is dead.

Pow! The hunters are done and put away their guns
Now the hunters have had their fun
But they don't know what they have done
To the animals that were made to run
But were shot down by a gun
The animals who lived will always remember what the
hunters did.

That cold December with fear in their eyes
They're getting more scared for the next sunrise
The morning is here and the hunters are near
Pow! The guns roar as blood covers the snow...

Jasmyn Morris-Holden (11)
St Joseph's RC High School & Sports College, Horwich

No Place You Can Go

Even though you may feel alone
There will always be others like you
No one to talk to, alone in your room
Online or at school, they are always around you.
No one can fully understand just how you feel
Faces all around, laughing and pointing
It can leave your life a misery
And there's nothing you can do
Teachers are not helpful
And parents stuck on what to do
Move to a different school
But it carries on day after day
There may be more awareness now
But it's still a lonely place
Bullying is an issue around the world
And if it happens to you
It might feel like there is no place you can go.

Amy Halliwell (12)
St Joseph's RC High School & Sports College, Horwich

Why Is Life Unfair?

Why is life unfair?
Why are there medical conditions
That take over people's lives?
They control them
What about young children in the hospital
And not playing outside?
They can't play with friends
It's not fair
They can't do what other kids their age do
What about children not being able
To do the job they want to do?
They are dying at young ages
All because of medical conditions
Children find it hard to be different
Why can't they have fun outside with friends?
Children are struggling with their lives
Why can't we help them more?
Why is life unfair?

Molly Scot-Walker (12)
St Joseph's RC High School & Sports College, Horwich

Best Friends

Best friends are forever
And nothing can break that apart
It's a part of your soul
And still, nothing and no one
Can break that apart.

It's as if a lock
Has been trapped around it
And can't break through
As if animals are trying
To escape a zoo.

It's a great feeling no one gets
Sometimes, relationships act like jets.

Times can be tough
Times can be rough.

Sometimes you ask yourself
"Why me? Why me?"

Don't be sad
And please don't be mad.

Things might change
If you read the right page.

Ben Shone (12)
St Joseph's RC High School & Sports College, Horwich

Fake A Smile

Every day, you fake a smile
You run to your room
Just to get away for a while
At school, everyone calls me names
Just to make me feel ashamed
There are also other people
Who feel the same.

You feel embarrassed
But too scared to say something
Because you think you're transparent.
You hit me, you kick me
But after I say, "What have I done?"
You hit me again and laugh in my face.

I have silence as a reply
Why am I getting punished
When I don't have a lot of courage?
I just wish it would stop
So, every day, I have to fake a smile.

Aaron Storey (12)
St Joseph's RC High School & Sports College, Horwich

Global Warming - A Killer

Why are we using carbon?
Why are we making floods happen?
Why are we causing Antarctica to die?
No point
No reason to do it
Electricity burning ice
Power stations are killing ice
Ice is water and when it melts
It can cause floods
Countries and islands will be covered with water
And will start disappearing
Warmth will defrost the Arctic
No space will be left
It will all be water
It is growing like a disease
We shouldn't do these things
Global warming is increasing faster now
Faster than the last century
There will be more water than sand...

Toby Runciman (13)
St Joseph's RC High School & Sports College, Horwich

Addiction

We all know the bad ones
The drugs and what they do
But no one ever notices the phone
The devil
The evil
It takes us away from family
It takes us away from friends
Overall, it's just addiction
"Wait, I'm typing."
We're slowly dying
Texting and driving
The worst mistake of all
You won't be laughing
When it takes the life from us all
Overall, it's just addiction
It's funny how these days
One-year-olds have tablets and phones
This society is a wonder
We all need a doctor
Overall, it's just addiction.

Amelka Zambrzycka (12)
St Joseph's RC High School & Sports College, Horwich

We Are All Unique

Stop it, stop it, stop it
What is the point?
Racism is where you bully someone
Because of the colour of their skin
What?

It's like being trapped
Inside a battleground
There are people who are upset.

I'm against racism
You know you shouldn't do it
They only want to fit

Stop it now, can't you see they're hurt?
They lock themselves away from the world
And cry.

Stop it, stop it, stop it
What is the point?
Racism is where you bully someone
Because of the colour of their skin
Why?

Libby Houghton (11)
St Joseph's RC High School & Sports College, Horwich

Better Than Them

People in this world always put you down
Ignore what they say!
You are important!
You are worth something.
Always have in your mind
That these bullies are jealous of you
You are important
You are worth something.

They are losers
You are a champion.

If you don't believe in yourself
Read and read this message
Over and over again
Because you are important
You are worth something.

There are many people in this world
Waiting to unlock the goodness inside you
Don't let them knock you down!

Joshua McMahon (13)
St Joseph's RC High School & Sports College, Horwich

Bullying Is Horrible

When people say names, it gives pain
The crying, the sorrow, the sadness
Anxiety creeping up as people are being mean to you
Bing! Bing! goes the phone
Horrible messages pile in
You give a shriek of help
But no one hears
The people who you thought were your friends
Turned out to be monsters...

Tell your teacher, parent or someone you trust
To stop the monsters hiding in the dust
Make new friends and have some fun
Forget everyone who hurt you
And enjoy your life
Bullying is unacceptable
So stop, stop, stop!

Ayeza Athar (12)
St Joseph's RC High School & Sports College, Horwich

Words Can Hurt

Words can hurt and can make me feel sad
Even when I said nothing bad
Sometimes, words that hurt the most
May just be a joke.

Every day I go to school
Where there are lots of fools
They push me to a wall
As they are very tall
They do it for attention
I hope they get detention.

It's all going well
Until some sharks jump out
And try to bite
There's no peace around here
Because they're all around.

Words can hurt
I don't know why
But all I know
Is that they make me cry.

Millie Jean Howarth (11)
St Joseph's RC High School & Sports College, Horwich

Lost Family Members

Yeah, it's hard living life without that one person
The one who brought you up
And helped you out in life.
That person has gone, but still in your heart
Living life without that missing part
You miss the person that you lost
And then, you go on your knees
And say, "Come back to me!
Why did you have to go?
We were friends, not foes!"
Family is your life and you can't afford to lose it
You have a hole in your heart
Days can be bad, especially birthdays and holidays
Don't get me started on the death day...

Josh Papp (12)
St Joseph's RC High School & Sports College, Horwich

It's Not About Looks

Don't judge a person by their cover
Like you wouldn't judge a book by its cover.
People who are bullied are haunted by words
It's like their lives are locked away
Waiting to be freed by something
Yet, they don't know what it is.

Corridors are battlegrounds
It is like everything is an obstacle
Every day, they are apprehensive to go to school
Every day, they hesitate when they do something
Every day, all they have are broken memories
Waiting to be healed.
That is their life
Hard, miserable, depressing.

Lujain Al Moukayed (12)
St Joseph's RC High School & Sports College, Horwich

Families

Families are like angels
They're always there
But you can't see them
They can make you feel happy
When they make you laugh
But they can also make you sad
Even if you have someone who was your parent
But they couldn't keep you
So then they put you up for adoption
But then you will have a parent
Who will always love you
And would love to have you
They will always be there for you, day and night
All families are kind and loving
But could also be a person
That would be like a best friend to you.

Lucy Sherratt (12)
St Joseph's RC High School & Sports College, Horwich

Family

Family is the best thing that will happen to you
Family needs all your time and love
Do you love your family?
You need to do special things to keep them close
Cherish your loved ones
Spend all your time with them to show the love that they need
Because, one day, they won't be there
You'll lie awake at night thinking to yourself
I should have made an effort.
I should have been there when they needed me
Keep your loved ones close
Because one day, they won't be there.

Olivia Rose Killeen (13)
St Joseph's RC High School & Sports College, Horwich

The Dark Web

Roses are red, violets are blue
Surfing the Web is entirely up to you
Are you safe?
Or are you in a trap?
You come across a user called 'cat in a cap'
He tries to be nice and overcome his tears
You compliment him, he laughs and says, "Cheers."
He says that you'll be friends for years and years
Is he your age or is he lying?
For you to fall for it, he is relying
Now, behind the screen, he is over the moon
Another harmless child to be led to their doom.

Callum O'Hanlon (12)
St Joseph's RC High School & Sports College, Horwich

What Are Friends?

What are friends?
Friends are the people who act fairly
Like brothers and sisters
Friends can be good
Some can be bad
Happy or sad
Mad or glad
They can be anything but fake.

Bad friends are fake
Good friends are real friends.

Fake friends don't care about you
They just want to dig inside you
And then turn around and bully you
Real friends care about you
And stand up for you
And never leave your side.

Amalia Vogt (11)
St Joseph's RC High School & Sports College, Horwich

The Dangers Of Social Media

Online bullying is a disgrace
We are all one, the human race
Racism is bad, really not funny
When you're the one being the bully
Now, get off stupid Facebook
And stand up to those who can't.

Facebook, Instagram, Snapchat and Twitter
Don't put on what you wouldn't say to their face.
Facebook, Instagram, Snapchat and Twitter
Fake news spreading like butter on toast.

So, watch out for the dangers of social media.

Leo Brannan (11)
St Joseph's RC High School & Sports College, Horwich

War

Bang! The bombs go off
The lights go off
The metallic birds see their prey
Then, they fire
Screams across the whole globe
Stop war, stop war.
No one cares if it isn't there
Why is violence the solution?
War should be stopped.

The red ball comes and kills
People run and hide, but always die
When will the Syrian war end?
Please stop war, please stop war
War kills our planet and life on Earth.

Alex Lloyd (12)
St Joseph's RC High School & Sports College, Horwich

In Afghanistan

In Afghanistan, where the war goes on
Where bodies lie, for what? Why?
Frightened families finding aid under threat of persecution
In Afghanistan, where bodies lie
Will their pain ever go away?
Burying bullets, injuring innocents as the wind kisses them
goodbye
The Reaper comes quickly,
The bombarding bombs destroy everything in their path
The buildings stand tall, watching suspiciously.

Edward Whittingham (13)
St Joseph's RC High School & Sports College, Horwich

Bullying

Bullying is a hurtful thing
Yet it still goes on

Bullying can hurt children
Around the world

Not just kids
But adults too

Bullying is wrong
And it needs to stop

Sadly, it still carries on

Bullying can make children
Move from school to school

Yet, children and adults
Think it's cool

So, stop bullying, please!

Jessica Hazel Stocks (12)
St Joseph's RC High School & Sports College, Horwich

Oh Pizza!

There's no point to life if I could never taste pepperoni
There's no point in living if I could never taste that beautiful
stuffed crust
There's no point to life if there's no jalapeños and juicy
cheese
Oh pizza, never could I live without you
That sweet taste when you chomp down
My tastebuds would be so lonely without you
How could I ever live without you?

Luke Leadbeater (12)
St Joseph's RC High School & Sports College, Horwich

Sports Are Healthy

Doing sport is healthy
Doing sport makes you strong and fit

Sports can make you lose weight
Even if you don't need to

You can do football when you're bored
And you can do it when you're out at a park
And you can play with family and friends

You can play football for so long
You can burn some energy
And have some fun all day long.

Sophie Patricia Stocks (12)
St Joseph's RC High School & Sports College, Horwich

Inequalities

Inequalities happen everywhere
But nobody knows
Everybody thinks that they are completely different
But they are blind to how much we are the same
Every day, they feel lonely because of the way they are
treated

People don't take notice of what society does to people
nowadays
Discrimination
Prejudice
Inequalities
These make people feel down.

Alisha McChrystal (13)
St Joseph's RC High School & Sports College, Horwich

You Are Amazing

You wake up
In puddles of tears and sweat
Your life is a disappointment
Why should you get out of bed?

But when you fall down
You have to learn how to get back up again
In life, you'll get doubted
So prove them wrong.

You are clever!
You're beautiful
You are worth it
Believe in yourself
Because you are amazing.

Benedict Kayonda (11)
St Joseph's RC High School & Sports College, Horwich

Family

Family isn't just your mum, dad, brothers and sisters
It includes your friends
They don't just come and go
They're always there
If they shout at you, it's for the best
They always care for you and what you want
They always put you first

If you're upset, give them a call
They won't be mad if you've done something bad.

Chloe Jones (12)
St Joseph's RC High School & Sports College, Horwich

Irlen Syndrome

Eleven years go on
Irlen's still goes on
I want to see my mum
But Irlen's still a bomb.

The light waves, blue and red
Distort all around my head
I want to see what you look like
But all you are is a blur.

It kills me day and night
And all around the page
Eleven years go on
And the page is still a blob.

Michael Anderton (11)
St Joseph's RC High School & Sports College, Horwich

How Would You Like It?

Yeah, it's hard living life
With people who are always bullying you
They don't stop, they think it's funny
When the reality is that it just hurts
Stop bullying, bullying is harmful
It ruins lives, makes lines, takes lives
It just hurts families
So, stop bullying
There is no point in hurting others.

Layton Openshaw (13)
St Joseph's RC High School & Sports College, Horwich

Bullying

Bullies aren't following rules at school
But know they need to act cool
Bullies are never-ending cruelty
Yet they don't know how to act cool
Bullying needs to move on
It makes kids move from schools
Yet, adults and kids think it's cool

Bullying is cruel and totally not cool.

Azuolas Sinusas (12)
St Joseph's RC High School & Sports College, Horwich

Friends

My friends mean the world to me
We hang around like monkeys in a tree

My friendship with them is special and true
We stick together like paper and glue

We meet at school
Where the girls rule

We sit in English class, gladly
Being taught my Mrs Bradley.

Molly Hacking (12)
St Joseph's RC High School & Sports College, Horwich

School

The world is a game
You think you're a loser
In the end
We are all the same

You don't have to be on top
Everyone around you loves you
We are all the shining spot

Stones can break bones
Words can break humanity
Hope and love is the key.

Greg Kay (13)
St Joseph's RC High School & Sports College, Horwich

A Vicious Cycle

In the early bright,
we prepare for a long day's fight.
We fix our bayonets and pray to God,
that we won't perish in a sea of mud.

Whilst our feet are stuck in an ocean of vermin and mire,
we sing like a church choir.
Suspense is hanging in the air,
as to who will meet their deaths over there.

The whistle blows and over the top we go,
if we ever return, that we don't yet know.
We hear the bullets whizzing past and the shells falling
down,
and yet we keep charging, as fellow men drown in seas of
blood.

Eventually, we get to it, what we've fought so hard for,
the enemy trench.
It is ghostly and deserted,
and there is quite a stench.

Then, the enemy come at us,
whole hordes of them, a giant grey cloud.
Then, our machine guns mow them down,
they are like bowling pins falling to the ground.

And, as the shadow of night falls,
the dogs of Flanders howl their calls.
We can see a pile of bodies, both khaki and grey,
and there they will forever stay.

There are not many of us left now,
even though this is the norm, it still surprises us somehow.
We think of the wives and mothers,
weeping at the deaths of their sons and brothers.

Tomorrow will be a repeat of today,
another murderous doomsday.
As on any other night, with a level of death that none can comprehend,
we ask, will it ever end?

Max Stuart Graham Gilmore (13)

Tarleton Academy, Tarleton

The Future

Empty streets
Unfilled houses
The danger of it all
Is known by us all
The intense sound
Of the factory coming down
Human arms, human brains
Are being replaced
Not by others, not even dogs
While we make, we create
The future of our own
The future of dolls becoming alive
The future of human hands
Being replaced by porcelain.

Nikola Zygo (16)
Thomas Whitham Sixth Form, Burnley

The Monster Under My Bed

You've taken it all
You've taken my freedom
My laugh
My smile
Me
At least
The way I used to be
Now, I lie awake every night
Tossing and turning
Afraid I'll meet another demon if I close my eyes.

You make me feel weak
You make me feel so alone
Yet I'm surrounded by so many people every day
You have taken so much from me
But I'm still here with everything
Well, almost everything.

You've torn me up inside
Broken me to pieces
You make me feel so suffocated, no matter where I am
You make me want to scream and shout
Until there's nothing left but silence
But I just can't.

I'm afraid.

I'm scared of what's to come
But I want today to be over
I want to say so much
But I'm afraid of what they'll think of me
I want to speak so many words
But I can't go against what's written
I want to skip these chapters
But I don't know when your time's over
I want to close this book
But I can't
Not yet
Because you have made me realise
That I am sleepwalking on an ocean of happiness
Because you are the monster under my bed.

Beatrix Neary-Taggart (13)
Turton High School, Bolton

Anxiety

Anxiety is something you can't control
It's something that won't go away like a headache or a
common cold
It's something that stays and never goes
Anxiety is a parasite which is stuck in your head
It's a parasite that is always telling you what it is
Yes, it may stop you from doing things that would take your
life
But anxiety can take lives
It takes away privileges that most people have
Like going out with your friends and being happy
It's something that makes people go from having a real
smile to a fake one
Anxiety keeps you up at night, staring at your ceiling,
worrying about nothing
Like that piece of homework you forgot to do
Or that plan you cancelled with your friend
It keeps you up, praying to God that it will go away
But all you get is silence
And that is something anxiety makes you do
Be silent!

Ava Longworth (12)
Turton High School, Bolton

The Rat

There is a rat
I call Depression
Inside me
Eating at my innards
The pain goes to my throat
So I am choking on my tears
My tears of blood
Would that I could
Write something else
I am so very tired
If only I could end it all
Looking at the words on the page
That reflect back to me my misery.

Charlie Holt (11)
Turton High School, Bolton

The True You

Labels don't define who you are
You're iridescent like a star
Black or white
Boy or girl
We'll all shine in the light

Prejudice and discrimination
It occurs in every nation
But what are we fighting for?

We all feel the same feelings
Think the same thoughts
Hindu or Christian
Indian or African
Female or male

All will conquer
Rich or poor
We all deserve more

We accept
When we should reject
Segregation
We could unite as one

Whoever you are
You are a star

It is not bizarre
To be who you are.

Tara Jessica Cummings (13)
Turton High School, Bolton

Bullying

Bullying, bullying, happening every day
Younger or older
Smaller or taller
Online or not.

People, people, crying every day
Loved by family, but hurt by others
Bullying causes this
No matter where they are.

Friends, friends, they leave, one by one
Calling names and hurting others
Everyone changes
But some for the worst, not the better.

Cyber, cyber, the click of a mouse
The tap of a keyboard can change everyone's life
Cyber or physical, they are both equally bad
Each one causes pain and strife.

Bullying, bullying, happening every day
Younger or older
Smaller or taller
Online or not.

Kayleigh Robinson (13)
Unity Academy, Blackpool

Boy

Boy, boy, unable to talk
People make fun of you
You love English
But you didn't believe you could do it
Listen to some music
And you will be fine
Become an English writer
And you will be divine.

Leah Carradice (13)
Unity Academy, Blackpool

YOUNG WRITERS INFORMATION

We hope you have enjoyed reading this book – and that you will continue to in the coming years.

If you're a young writer who enjoys reading and creative writing, or the parent of an enthusiastic poet or story writer, do visit our website **www.youngwriters.co.uk**. Here you will find free competitions, workshops and games, as well as recommended reads, a poetry glossary and our blog. There's lots to keep budding writers motivated to write!

If you would like to order further copies of this book, or any of our other titles, then please give us a call or visit **www.youngwriters.co.uk**.

Young Writers
Remus House
Coltsfoot Drive
Peterborough
PE2 9BF
(01733) 890066
info@youngwriters.co.uk

Join in the conversation!
Tips, news, giveaways and much more!

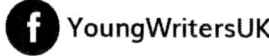 **YoungWritersUK**    **@YoungWritersCW**